Self-Defending Ne
The Next Generation of Ne

Duane De Capite

Cisco Press

800 East 96th Street
Indianapolis, IN 46240 USA

Self-Defending Networks
The Next Generation of Network Security

Duane De Capite

Copyright© 2007 Cisco Systems, Inc.

Published by:
Cisco Press
800 East 96th Street
Indianapolis, IN 46240 USA

Printed in the United States of America 1 2 3 4 5 6 7 8 9 0

First Printing September 2006

Library of Congress Cataloging-in-Publication Number: 2005932409

ISBN: 1-58705-253-9

Warning and Disclaimer

This book is designed to provide information about self-defending networks. Every effort has been made to make this book as complete and as accurate as possible, but no warranty or fitness is implied.

The information is provided on an "as is" basis. The authors, Cisco Press, and Cisco Systems, Inc., shall have neither liability nor responsibility to any person or entity with respect to any loss or damages arising from the information contained in this book or from the use of the discs or programs that may accompany it.

The opinions expressed in this book belong to the author and are not necessarily those of Cisco Systems, Inc.

Feedback Information

At Cisco Press, our goal is to create in-depth technical books of the highest quality and value. Each book is crafted with care and precision, undergoing rigorous development that involves the unique expertise of members from the professional technical community.

Readers' feedback is a natural continuation of this process. If you have any comments regarding how we could improve the quality of this book, or otherwise alter it to better suit your needs, you can contact us through e-mail at feedback@ciscopress.com. Please be sure to include the book title and ISBN in your message.

We greatly appreciate your assistance.

Corporate and Government Sales

Cisco Press offers excellent discounts on this book when ordered in quantity for bulk purchases or special sales.

For more information please contact: **U.S. Corporate and Government Sales** 1-800-382-3419 corpsales@pearsontechgroup.com

For sales outside the U.S. please contact: **International Sales** international@pearsoned.com

Dedications

This book is dedicated to Donna, Nicolas, and Annabella: Thank you for making all of my dreams come true.

Acknowledgments

I am very fortunate to work with lots of great people. These people have helped me with insight and by answering all of my many questions. I am also fortunate to have lots of support from people at work as well as at home. This support has enabled me to write this book, and I am very thankful for this opportunity.

This book would not have been possible without the support from my family. It took a long time to write, and I had to promise that I would not start writing another book for at least six months. The process required many long evenings and weekends, and special thanks goes to my wife Donna for providing inspiration, writing feedback, and encouraging me throughout.

I would like to thank the reviewers, Darrin Miller and Chris Tobkin, for the excellent job and contributions to this book. I would also like to thank Denise Helfrich for authoring portions of this book while managing to coauthor another book for Cisco Press. I would also like to thank the excellent editorial staff at Cisco Press. This book would not be possible without the contributions by Brett Bartow and Dayna Isley.

Dozens of people helped me by answering questions and providing access to equipment. Special thanks goes these individuals, including Nick Chong, Edmund Lam, Steven Lee, Mark Bernier, Francesca Martucci, Steve DeJarnett, Joshua Houston, and Hari Shankar.

I would also like to thank the leadership team in the Security Technology Group for its support and guidance over the years. Special thanks goes to Amrit Patel and Dario Zamarian for giving me the opportunity to work with many of the great product teams in the Security Technology Group and for giving me the opportunity to write this book.

This Book Is Safari Enabled

The Safari® Enabled icon on the cover of your favorite technology book means the book is available through Safari Bookshelf. When you buy this book, you get free access to the online edition for 45 days.

Safari Bookshelf is an electronic reference library that lets you easily search thousands of technical books, find code samples, download chapters, and access technical information whenever and wherever you need it.

To gain 45-day Safari Enabled access to this book:

- Go to http://www.ciscopress.com/safarienabled
- Complete the brief registration form
- Enter the coupon code 5TJG-RZDK-9FH2-4GKP-IVEK

If you have difficulty registering on Safari Bookshelf or accessing the online edition, please e-mail customer-service@safaribooksonline.com.

Contents at a Glance

Contents

Icons Used in This Book

Communication Server

PC

PC with Software

Sun Workstation

Macintosh

Access Server

ISDN/Frame Relay Switch

Token Ring

Terminal

File Server

Web Server

Ciscoworks Workstation

ATM Switch

Modem

Printer

Laptop

IBM Mainframe

Front End Processor

Cluster Controller

Multilayer Switch

Gateway

Router

Bridge

Hub

DSU/CSU

FDDI

Catalyst Switch

Network Cloud

Line: Ethernet

Line: Serial

Line: Switched Serial

DDoS Detector

PIX Right

Network Management Appliance

CiscoSecurity Manager

DDoS Guard

ASA (Active) CSC Module for Anti-Virus

Catalyst with Firewall Module and NAC

Router with IOS Firewall

NetRanger

Wireless Access Point (Authenticator)

Command Syntax Conventions

The conventions used to present command syntax in this book are the same conventions used in the IOS Command Reference. The Command Reference describes these conventions as follows:

- **Boldface** indicates commands and keywords that are entered literally as shown. In actual configuration examples and output (not general command syntax), boldface indicates commands that are manually input by the user (such as a **show** command).
- *Italics* indicate arguments for which you supply actual values.
- Vertical bars (l) separate alternative, mutually exclusive elements.
- Square brackets [ ] indicate optional elements.
- Braces { } indicate a required choice.
- Braces within brackets [{ }] indicate a required choice within an optional element.

Foreword

At Cisco, we strive to turn security from a silo and reactive approach to a proactive and holistic system that provides adaptive layers of defense-in-depth. Increasingly, network attacks are not just "outside-in" at the perimeter but "inside-out," necessitating threat protection and mitigation at every layer. Threats are taking vile and virulent forms and have turned from mere annoyances to menacing and significant losses of millions of dollars to businesses.

In this book, *Self Defending Networks: The Next Generation of Network Security,* the author Duane De Capite reviews not only the different forms of threats and protection, but he also examines the importance of architecting systematic network and information security. The need for risk mitigation, integrating innovative network security technologies such as unified threat management, behavioral day-zero protection, and application security with appropriate monitoring and control, is what makes networks truly *self-defending*. Such an architecture is not possible with point-products only. It calls for dramatic change from the band-aid approach to a thoughtful combination of policy, process, and technology. The author highlights the paramount importance of bridging the gap between classical desktop antivirus options and network security. Network administrators must have plans to integrate security seamlessly into their networks and build more collaborative trust models with Network Admission Control (NAC) across Cisco internetworks and industrywide coalitions and standards.

As we build networks of the 21st century deploying mobile devices, real-time video interactions, Internet telephony, and web applications, it is clear that security can no longer be an afterthought but is at the forefront of all new deployments. I do hope you will enjoy reading and learning the various attributes of security products and technologies that transform self-defending networks to the *reality* of securing information assets, applications, and networks.

Jayshree Ullal
Senior Vice President, Security, Switching and Datacenter Technologies
Cisco Systems

Introduction

Security is one of the fastest-growing areas in the networking and IT industries today. Security is often the top concern of Chief Information Officers (CIOs) and one of the top technology initiatives of many organizations. However, security projects often do not get the focus needed to be approved and deployed. Perhaps, this reticence can be explained by the complexity of security. Cisco has reduced the cost to deploy and manage security by creating a self-defending network. The self-defending network can enable the network to detect and defend itself against certain attacks. This book provides an overview of the attacks that a self-defending network can protect against, introduces the components of a self-defending network, and details how an organization can manage its self-defending network in a centralized and integrated fashion.

This book provides an overview of the components of a self-defending network, including distributed denial-of-service (DDoS) mitigation, Adaptive Security Appliances (ASA), Cisco Incident Control Service (Cisco ICS), NAC framework, NAC appliances (Cisco Clean Access), IEEE 802.1x, Cisco Security Agent (CSA), and integrated, centralized management.

Management is the glue that enables the components of a self-defending network to integrate and share a common defensive plan to thwart network attacks. The Cisco Security Manager and Cisco Security MARS are the bedrock of the Cisco centralized management strategy.

Goals and Methods

The goal of this book is to familiarize you with concepts, benefits, and implementation details of a Cisco self-defending network. This book endeavors to make you more comfortable with the following topics:

- Security threats and risks to IP networks
- Baseline security components of a traditional security network
- Concepts and benefits of a Cisco self-defending network
- Advanced topics in network security, including DDoS mitigation, NAC, and 802.1x
- In-depth coverage of the Cisco centralized management suite, including the Cisco Security Manager and Cisco Security MARS.

This book is not intended to be a one-stop shopping destination or a step-by-step guide to deploy each component of a self-defending network; instead, this book is a first-step to introduce you to the components of the Cisco self-defending network. If this book were a menu item in a restaurant, it would be a sampler platter, not an all-you-can buffet or a complete five-course meal. You can read this book in a day and, in that time, gain the ability to discuss the philosophy and components of a self-defending network at a high-level.

This book is heavily focused on device management and centralized management to show how you can manage a self-defending network. Many chapters of this book contain screenshots from beta or alpha software to get this book to market shortly after the products are released. There may be changes in the device manager and centralized management GUIs from alpha/beta software. There may also be changes in the device managers and centralized management GUIs between the versions used in the book and subsequent versions that are released to the market after the publication of this book.

Who Should Read This Book?

This book is intended for everyone learning about security and next-generation security networks, including Chief Security Officers (CSOs) and CIOs, network engineers and architects, and engineering students. This book is written to enable quick overview coverage of topics like DDoS, while creating a quick reference to enable deep-dives into specific implementation details, like how to deploy an 802.1x network.

How This Book Is Organized

This book is designed to be read as a beginning-to-intermediate overview of Cisco self-defending networks. The chapters cover the following topics:

- **Chapter 1, "Understanding Types of Network Attacks and Defenses"**—Starts with an overview of network security threats and then details specific components of a self-defending network.

- **Chapter 2, "Mitigating Distributed Denial-of-Service Attacks"**—Discusses the DDoS attack threats to an IP network and the components to mitigate this DDoS thread, including the DDoS service module for the Catalyst 6500/7600 family and the DDoS Device Manager.

- **Chapter 3, "Cisco Adaptive Security Appliance Overview"**—Discusses the Cisco security appliance for firewall, IPS, VPN, antivirus, antispam, antiphishing, and URL filtering. This chapter also details how you can use the Adaptive Security Appliance Device Manager (ASDM) to help create a self-defending network.

- **Chapter 4, "Cisco Incident Control Service"**—Examines the Cisco ICS product, developed with Trend Micro, that enables IOS routers, IPS Sensors, and the IPS module (AIP-SSM) of the Adaptive Security Appliance to update virus-related IPS signatures. This chapter also details the ability of Cisco ICS to configure access-list rules on IOS routers and ASA security appliances to help to protect the network against network virus infections.

- **Chapter 5, "Demystifying 802.lx"**—Examines the underlying technology of the IEEE 802.1x standard, which enables networks to identify, authenticate, and authorize users to the desired VLANs and applications. This chapter also details how 802.1x can be a component of NAC.

- **Chapter 6, "Implementing Network Admission Control"**—Provides an overview of the component of a self-defending network that authenticates and quarantines rogue users and users with down-level versions of OS patches and virus-protecting software. This chapter is dedicated to NAC framework, or a NAC solution that uses existing routers and switches.

- **Chapter 7, "Network Admission Control Appliance"**—Covers the fundamentals of and configuration of the NAC appliance (Cisco Clean Access) product line. Specifically, this chapter covers how this NAC appliance can provide an alternative to the embedded components of NAC framework that may be attractive to several target markets, including the education market. This chapter also details how 802.1x is not required to implement NAC with the NAC appliance.

- **Chapter 8, "Managing the Cisco Security Agent"**—Covers the fundamentals and configuration of the end-point or desktop self-defending component. It also discusses the product to provide end-point or desktop protection for up to 100,000 PCs or laptops with a single management center.

- **Chapter 9, "Cisco Security Manager"**—Covers the centralized management product (Cisco Security Manager), which can configure the self-defending network for routers, switches, ASA, and IPS devices. This chapter also details how a management station can manage a self-defending network.

- **Chapter 10, "Cisco Security Monitoring, Analysis, and Response System"**—Details how Cisco Security MARS can centrally monitor and provide mitigation for a self-defending network. Cisco Security MARS received monitoring input from many components in the self-defending network, including routers, switches, ASA devices, IPS devices, databases, hosts, and Cisco Security Agents.

CHAPTER 1

Understanding Types of Network Attacks and Defenses

Reports of network security attacks have been increasing at an alarming rate. These network attacks fall into a variety of categories, none of them being attractive things that you want on your network. Network uptime, online orders, and productivity from networked applications are your offense, or networked assets. Network security is your defense, or protection of your networked assets, from these ever-increasing network attacks. A self-defending network is the next generation of network security, which introduces a new, innovative security architecture that can provide an additional layer of protection against network attacks.

Categorizing Network Attacks

Network attacks can be categorized based upon the nature of the attack. Categories of network attacks include the following:

- Virus
- Worm
- Trojan Horse
- Denial of service (DoS)
- Distributed denial of service (DDoS)
- Spyware
- Phishing

The next sections describe each of these categories in more detail.

Virus

When I was a software developer for a large systems company in the early 1990s, one of my coworkers liked to tell a story about how his grandmother called him up one day at the office and told him that she was worried about his health because she was concerned that he would catch a computer virus and become sick! A tremendous amount of education and socialization about computer viruses has occurred since the early 1990s. Even television and radio advertisements talk about how Internet services come bundled with antivirus protection to thwart these dastardly viruses. As my coworker had to explain to his grandmother, only computers, not people, can catch these particular viruses.

The term *virus* is credited to University of Southern California professor Frederick Cohen in his 1984 research paper *Computer Viruses: Theory and Experiments*. A computer virus is designed to attack a computer and often to wreak havoc on other computers and network devices. A virus can often be an attachment in an e-mail, and selecting the attachment can cause the executable code to run and replicate the virus. Other examples of executable code that can contain a virus include spreadsheet macros, JavaScript, or a macro in a Microsoft Word document.

Simple text files and .JPG pictures for example do not spread viruses because they are treated as a data form to be viewed and are not executed by the target computer. A virus must be executed or run in memory in order to run and search for other programs or hosts to infect and replicate. As the name implies, a virus needs a host such as a spreadsheet or e-mail in order to attach, infect, and replicate.

There are several common effects of a virus. Some viruses are benign, and simply notify their victim that they have been infected. Viruses can also be malignant and create destruction by deleting files and otherwise wreaking havoc on the infected computer that contains digital assets, such as pictures, documents, passwords, and financial records.

Worm

In this case, *worm* doesn't refer to a hole in the space-time continuum. A *worm* is a destructive software program that scans for vulnerabilities or security holes on other computers in order to exploit the weakness and replicate.

Worms can replicate independently and very quickly. For example, in 2001, the Code Red worm replicated itself over 250,000 times in less than 12 hours. Worms can also be relatively small in size. The SQL Slammer worm from 2003, for example, was only around 400 bytes. Worms can also attack instant messaging technology, as evidenced by an alert from Trend Micro on the Bropia worm, which you can read about at ZDNet (http://news.zdnet.com/2100-1009_22-5562129.html).

NOTE   Two researchers at Xerox Parc are credited with developing the first computer worm in 1978.

Worms differ from viruses in two major ways:

- Viruses require a host to attach and execute, and worms do not require a host.
- Viruses and worms typically cause different types of destruction.

Viruses, once they are resident in memory, often delete and modify important files on the infected computer. Worms, however, tend to be more network-centric than computer-centric. Worms can replicate quickly by initiating network connections to replicate and send massive amounts of data. Worms, such as SQL Slammer, brought many unsuspecting networks to their knees by initiating large numbers of network connections and data transfers. This type of network attack is also called a *distributed denial-of-service (DDoS)* attack, which is discussed in more detail later in this chapter.

Worms can also contain a piggybacked passenger, or data payload, which can relegate a target computer to the status of a zombie. A *zombie* is a computer that has been compromised and is now under control by the network attacker. Zombies are often used to launch additional network attacks. A large collection of zombies under the control of an attacker is referred to as a "botnet." Botnets can grow to be quite large. Botnets have been identified that were larger than 100,000 zombie computers.

Trojan Horse

A Trojan horse, or Trojan, is pernicious software that attempts to masquerade itself as a trusted application such as a game or screen saver. Once the unsuspecting user attempts to access what appears to be an innocuous game or screen saver, the Trojan can initiate damaging activities such as deleting files or reformatting a hard drive. Trojans are typically not self-replicating.

Network attackers attempt to use popular applications, such as Apple's iTunes, to deploy a Trojan. For example, a network attack sends an e-mail with a purported link to download a free iTunes song. This Trojan would then initiate a connection to an external web server and initiate an attack once the user attempted to download the apparent free song.

Denial-of-Service

A denial-of-service (DoS) attack is a network attack that results in the denial of service by a requested application such as a web server. There are several mechanisms to generate a DoS attack. The simplest method is to generate large amounts of what appears to be valid network traffic. This type of network DoS attack attempts to clog the network pipe so that valid user traffic cannot get through the network connection. However, this type of DoS typically needs to be distributed because it usually requires more than one source to generate the attack (more on distributed DoS, or DDoS, attacks in the following section).

A DoS attack takes advantage of the fact that target systems such as servers must maintain state information and may have expected buffer sizes and network packet contents for specific applications. A DoS can exploit this vulnerability by sending packet sizes and data values that are not expected by the receiving application.

Several types of DoS attacks exist, including Teardrop attacks and the Ping of Death, which send handcrafted network packets that are different from those the application expects and may provoke the application and server to crash. These DoS attacks on an unprotected server, such as an ecommerce server, can cause the server to crash and prevent users from adding items to their shopping cart.

Distributed Denial-of-Service

A DDoS is similar in intent of a DoS attack, except that a DDoS attack originates from multiple source attack points. In addition to increasing the amount of network traffic from multiple, distributed attackers, a DDoS attack also presents the challenge of requiring the network defense to identify and stop each of the distributed attackers. You learn more about DDoS attacks in the section "DDoS Mitigation."

Several years ago, I was on a customer site visit to a very large online retailer at the very same time they were under a DDoS attack. They were able to stop the DDoS attack without dedicated DDoS mitigation products, but a significant amount of time was involved to identify the sources of the attack. This investigation, as well as the eventual remediation of the attack, involved communication and cooperation from the customer's Internet service provider (ISP). The intended victim was able to stop the attack after several hours, but they also had to stop the flow of valid traffic (in this case sales orders) in order to stop the DDoS attack.

Spyware

Spyware is a class of software applications that can participate in a network attack. Spyware is an application that attempts to install and remain hidden on a target PC or laptop. Once the spyware application has been surreptitiously installed, the spyware captures information about what users are doing with their computers. Some of this captured information includes websites visited, e-mails sent, and passwords used. Attackers can use the captured passwords and information to gain entry to a network to launch a network attack.

In addition to being used to directly participate in a network attack, Spyware can also be used to gather information that can be sold underground. This information, once purchased, can be used by another attacker that is "harvesting data" to be used in planning another network attack.

Phishing

Phishing is a type of network attack that typically starts by sending an e-mail to an unsuspecting user. The phishing e-mail attempts to look like a legitimate e-mail from a known and trusted institution such as a bank or ecommerce site. This false e-mail attempts to convince users that something has happened, such as suspicious activity on their account, and that the user must follow the link in the e-mail and logon to the site to view their user information. The link in this e-mail is often a false copy of the real bank or ecommerce site and features a similar look-and-feel to the real site. The phishing attack is designed to trick users into providing valuable information such as their username and password.

Understanding Traditional Network Defenses

Traditional security networks rely heavily on router access lists, firewalls, and intrusion detection to protect the network against attacks. These products provide a good baseline for network security; however, you can supplement them with other security products to increase network security. These traditional network security products are also typically manually configured, often with different administrators and different graphical user interfaces (GUIs).

The remainder of this chapter discusses traditional network defenses and provides an overview of a self-defending network. This chapter also describes how integrated, centralized management can help to increase network security. Figure 1-1 shows a network with traditional network defense components.

Figure 1-1   *Traditional Network Defense*

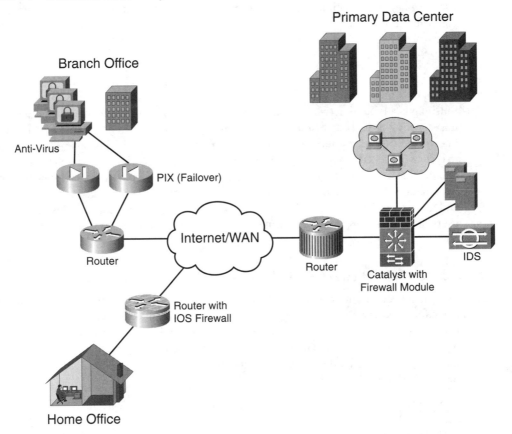

Traditional network defenses are composed of the following products, which you will learn more about in the next sections:

- Router access lists
- Firewalls
- Intrusion Detection Systems (IDS)
- Virtual Private Networks (VPNs)
- Antivirus programs

Router Access Lists

The access list, or access control list (ACL), is the cornerstone of network security. Access lists permit or deny network traffic based upon parameters including source IP address, destination IP address, and network service or port number. Router access lists are typically stateless, meaning that the router does not a maintain TCP connection state for each connection. Router access lists offer perimeter protection and a base defense because routers are typically both edge devices for perimeter networks and core devices for large networks. In addition to protecting edge and core networks, access lists are also often used to protect the network device itself.

Firewalls

Firewalls are prevalent in perimeter networks and data centers. Firewalls are often found in the perimeter to protect remote sites or edge networks. Network firewalls take their name from the traditional firewalls that can exist on trains and buildings to quarantine or block a fire from spreading from one area to another.

Network firewalls often follow a similar approach by protecting parts of the network from other parts of the network in the event of an attack. Firewalls maintain a TCP state for each connection that passes through the firewall. Firewalls can prevent attacked web servers or zombies from attacking other parts of the network. Network firewalls can also implement a demilitarized zone (DMZ) functionality. Portions or areas of the network can be classified as either outside the network, typically toward the Internet, or inside the network, typically toward the users or servers, or a DMZ. DMZs enable a layer of protection between the untrusted, in this case the outside of the network, and the trusted, or inside, part of the network. Router access lists and firewalls combine to compose the bedrock of traditional network security defenses.

Intrusion Detection Systems

Router access lists and firewalls have been pervasive since the early 1990s. Intrusion detection systems (IDSs) started to become widely deployed toward the end of the 1990s. IDSs are passive devices that monitor a copy of network traffic as it flows through the system. IDSs are often deployed in data centers near critical servers. As the name implies, these IDSs can detect a network attack based upon network traffic signatures or patterns of data in the network traffic.

IDSs typically detect rather than prevent the network attack because they are not inline, as they are operating on a copy of the network traffic. IDSs are highly valuable to network security defense, because they can provide an early warning that a network attack has been initiated.

Virtual Private Networks

VPNs are commonplace in most corporate networks. VPNs are essentially a security layer applied to a public or private network to make the network connection secure. VPNs are also considered to be leased-line or ISDN replacements. VPNs use authentication mechanisms including one-time passwords and encryption such as 3DES (Triple DES, pronounced "dez") or Advanced Encryption Standard (AES) to provide a secure layer on top of a network connection. Because VPNs often replace leased-lines like T1s or ISDN connections, they are often managed by the Network Operations group, or NetOps, rather than the Security Operations, or SecOPs, group. VPNs are not a major focus of this book as they are often managed by the NetOps group for a site-to-site connection or a remote access connection to the corporate data center.

Antivirus Programs

Many organizations have implemented an antivirus program to combat the frequent virus attacks against their network. Antivirus programs often scan received e-mail to identify and remove known virus attacks. While antivirus scanning components are valuable additions to the security of a network, antivirus components are traditionally standalone and not integrated into the network fabric. The ability to embed the antivirus functionality directly into a network enables the network to be self-defending as the security components can be integrated and centrally managed and provides a mechanism for the network to be self-healing and automatically defend itself against certain viruses or viral attacks.

Introducing Cisco Self-Defending Networks

Self-defending networks augment and complement the traditional network defense components outlined in the previous section. Self-defending networks differ from traditional network defenses in that self-defending networks have the capability to provide some amount of automatic protection of the network components and end-user workstations in the event of a network attack.

Self-defending networks can also be implemented in layers, in a manner similar to defensive layers of a football or soccer team. The layered self-defending network includes components that can protect the network connections in the data center, at the remote or branch location, and at the desktop. Self-defending networks can either recommend a configuration or automatically apply a configuration to prevent certain network attacks. Self-defending network components include the following:

- DDoS mitigation, including DDoS Guard and DDoS Traffic Anomaly Detector
- Adaptive Security Appliances (ASA)
- Incident Control Service (ICS)
- Network Admission Control (NAC)

- 802.1x
- Host intrusion prevention: Cisco Security Agent (CSA)
- Cisco Security Centralized management

Figure 1-2 displays an example of a network diagram with self-defending components. The next sections describe the components in more detail.

Figure 1-2 *Self-Defending Network*

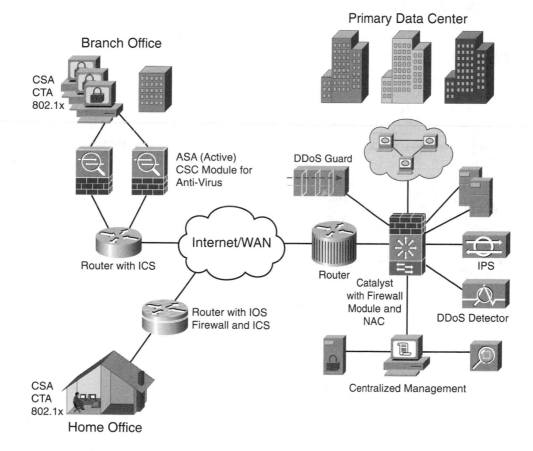

DDoS Mitigation

DDoS attacks can often be among the toughest to defend because they involve large amounts of what appears to be legitimate source traffic and multiple, distributed senders of this source traffic. Automatic or self-defending DDoS mitigation involves the automatic rerouting of the DDoS traffic while maintaining the valid network traffic connections. Cisco Guard and Detector appliances and Catalyst 6500/7600 DDoS service modules can provide this automatic DDoS mitigation by creating a baseline of normal network activity, detecting DDoS attacks and then automatically rerouting the DDoS traffic away from the target servers by updating the routing tables.

In addition to customer-managed DDoS mitigation solutions, there are also ISP-managed DDoS mitigation or clean-pipe solutions. These ISP-managed solutions are implemented with Cisco DDoS mitigation appliances and service modules. The ISP-managed solutions often contain partner products from Arbor Networks, which complement the Cisco DDoS mitigation appliance and linecard products.

Intrusion Prevention Systems

Intrusion Prevention Systems (IPSs) are the successor to IDS products. IDS operates on a copy of network traffic, from a source such as a span port on a LAN switch, so it can detect, but typically cannot prevent, an attack because the original network traffic has already propagated through the network.

IPS operates inline and processes the actual network packet, not a copy of the network traffic. IPSs can detect a network attack based upon network traffic signatures or patterns of data in the network traffic. Since IPS operates inline, IPS has the ability to drop the packets of the attack and prevent a network attack rather than detect a network attack. IPS is an important part of the self-defending network, rather than a traditional network defense, since IPS has the ability to be self-defending and prevent a network attack without manual operator intervention during the attack.

IPS can be implemented as a standalone IPS appliance or service module. IPS can also be implemented as an integrated component with the Adaptive Security Appliance (ASA). This book focuses on IPS as an integrated component with ASA rather than as a standalone product.

Adaptive Security Appliance

ASA is an integrated and extensible security appliance product line from Cisco. ASA is an integration of the PIX firewall, Network IDS/IPS system, and VPN 3000 concentrator. This ASA appliance contains many self-defending characteristics including inline IPS support, application layer inspection/enforcement, and SYN Cookie capabilities. These self-defending features can enable the ASA appliance to drop network attack connections and protect end servers and users from attacks by monitoring, inspecting, and restricting the network connection attempts to target devices. For example, the HTTP application inspection engine in ASA can inspect a specific HTTP connection flow and can drop an HTTP packet that does not conform to the proper packet format. The ASA IPS engine also allows specific IPS signatures to be applied to specific traffic flows. The inline IPS signature engine in ASA can be configured to automatically drop any packets in the traffic flow that match the IPS signature.

CHAPTER 2

Mitigating Distributed Denial-of-Service Attacks

The Cisco distributed denial-of-service (DDoS) mitigation solution is composed of two key components: Cisco Traffic Anomaly Detector, which is responsible for detecting a DDoS attack, and Cisco Guard, which is responsible for mitigating the attack. Customers can implement a DDoS solution with the Cisco Guard and the Cisco Traffic Anomaly Detector, or they can purchase the DDoS solution from a service provider. The solution from a service provider is often called a *clean pipes* solution. A clean pipes solution is implemented with a variety of products, including the Cisco Guard, Cisco Traffic Anomaly Detector, and partner products from vendors like Arbor Networks.

The Cisco Guard and the Cisco Traffic Anomaly Detector are based upon the patented Multi-Verification Process (MVP) architecture. This MVP architecture enables the Cisco Guard and Cisco Traffic Anomaly Detector to leverage the latest analysis and attack recognition techniques to detect and remove network attack traffic while scrubbing and reinjecting valid network traffic to its proper destination. Before describing the functions and configuration processes for these products, this chapter summarizes various DDoS attacks.

Understanding Types of DDoS Attacks

Table 2-1 describes several varieties of generic DDoS attacks.

Table 2-1   *Generic DDoS Attacks*

Name of Attack	Flooding Capability	Short Description
Land	TCP SYN	Source and destination IP addresses are the same, causing the TCP response to loop.
SYN	TCP	Sends large numbers of TCP connection initiation requests to the target. The target system must consume resources to keep track of these partially opened connections.
Teardrop	TCP fragments	Sends overlapping IP fragments.

continues

Table 2-1 *Generic DDoS Attacks (Continued)*

Name of Attack	Flooding Capability	Short Description
Smurf	Internet Control Message Protocol (ICMP)	Sends ICMP ping requests to a directed broadcast address. The forged source address of the request is the target of the attack. The recipients of the directed broadcast ping request respond to the request and flood the target's network.
Ping of death	ICMP	Brings down a system by sending out more than 65536 ICMP packets.
Open/close	TCP, UDP	Opens and closes connections at a high rate to any port serviced by an external service through inetd. The number of connections allowed is hard coded inside inetd (Internet super daemon, often used to run other services like FTP).
ICMP Unreachable	ICMP	The attacker sends ICMP unreachable packets from a spoofed address to a host. This causes all legitimate TCP connections on the host to be torn down to the spoofed address. This causes the TCP session to retry, and as more ICMP unreachables are sent, a denial-of-service (DoS) condition occurs.
ICMP redirect	ICMP	Causes data overload to the system being targeted.
ICMP Router Discovery Protocol (IRDP)	ICMP	Spoofing IRDP causes fake routing entries to be entered into a Windows machine. IRDP has no authentication. Upon startup, a system running MS Windows 95/98 will always send 3 ICMP Router Solicitation packets to the 224.0.0.2 multicast address. If the machine is NOT configured as a DHCP client, it ignores any Router Advertisements sent back to the host. However, if the Windows machine is configured as a DHCP client, any Router Advertisements sent to the machine will be accepted and processed.
ARP redirect	ARP	Attacks local subnets.
Looping User Datagram Protocol (UDP) ports	UDP	Spoofs two UDP services—chargen (port 19) and echo (port 7)—to send data to each other.
Fraggle	UDP	Same as Smurf, but uses UDP rather than ICMP to broadcast address for amplification.

Table 2-1   *Generic DDoS Attacks (Continued)*

Name of Attack	Flooding Capability	Short Description
UDP flood	UDP	Sends large numbers of UDP packets to the target system, thus tying up network resources.
TCP flood	TCP	Repeatedly establishes and abandons TCP connections, enabling a malicious host to tie up significant resources on a server.
UDP reflectors	UDP	All web servers, Domain Name System (DNS) servers, and routers are reflectors, because they will return SYN ACKs or RSTs in response to SYN or other TCP packets; query replies in response to query requests; or ICMP Time Exceeded or Host Unreachable in response to particular IP packets. By spoofing IP addresses from slaves, a massive DDoS attack can be arranged.
URL attacks	TCP	Attempts to overload an HTTP server with HTTP bombing (continuous requests for the same homepage or large web page) or by requesting the page with REFRESH to bypass any proxy server. Many of these attacks are not zombie attacks but rather human executed—by hundreds simultaneously.
Virtual Private Network (VPN) attacks	TCP	Using specially crafted Generic Routing Encapsulation (GRE) or IP in IP tunnel (IPIP) packets to attack the destination address of a VPN.

Source: Cisco Systems, Inc.

DDoS Mitigation Overview

To mitigate DDoS attacks, Cisco offers the Traffic Anomaly Detector and the Guard.

The Traffic Anomaly Detector learns what is a normal traffic pattern for a protected network area, or zone. After the Traffic Anomaly Detector establishes a network traffic baseline, DDoS mitigation policies are constructed and thresholds are tuned in order to configure the Traffic Anomaly Detector to react to various DDoS attack scenarios. In the event of a DDoS attack, the Traffic Anomaly Detector informs the Guard of the DDoS attack. The Guard diverts the traffic from the DDoS attack to the Guard. This DDoS attack diversion is typically implemented by updating the Border Gateway Protocol (BGP) routing table or by other mechanisms including static routes (manual IP routes) and policy-based routes (specific traffic forwarding based upon parameters including application and packet size).

The Guard's ability to update routing tables in the event of an attack allows the Guard to automatically scrub the DDoS attack traffic, while still forwarding or tunneling valid network traffic to the destination zone. The Traffic Anomaly Detector is often deployed upstream from the servers that are being protected in the data center. Figure 2-1 shows the Traffic Anomaly Detector and Guard appliances.

Figure 2-1   *Traffic Anomaly Detector and Guard Appliances*

Cisco Guard XT 5650 Appliance

Cisco Traffic Anomaly Detector XT 5600 Appliance

Source: Cisco Systems, Inc.

Using Cisco Traffic Anomaly Detector

The two main product options for the Cisco Traffic Anomaly Detector are the appliance and the Traffic Anomaly Detector service module on the Catalyst 6500 and Catalyst 7600 product lines. Figure 2-2 shows the Traffic Anomaly Detector service module.

Figure 2-2   *Catalyst 6500/7600 Traffic Anomaly Detector Service Module*

Source: Cisco Systems, Inc.

In addition to the Traffic Anomaly Detector, there are several others mechanisms to detect a DDoS attack and inform the Guard of the attack. Some of these mechanisms that detect a DDoS attack and inform the Guard include the DDoS signatures on the intrusion prevention system (IPS) appliances and modules. However, this section focuses on the Traffic Anomaly Detector because this component is frequently deployed and is a very feature-rich component for DDoS mitigation.

The Traffic Anomaly Detector is capable of monitoring gigabit speeds and operates on a copy of the network traffic. This copy of the network traffic is often obtained by using a span port of the Catalyst LAN switch to create a copy of the network traffic. The Traffic Anomaly Detector is designed to monitor the traffic destined to one of more zones. A Zone is a particular server, group of servers, subnet, network, or Internet service provider (ISP) that is being protected from a DDoS attack. The Traffic Anomaly Detector protects a zone by learning the baseline traffic destined to the zone, and then applies policy configuration and threshold tuning to protect the zone from a DDoS attack. The Traffic Anomaly Detector can be configured with command-line interface (CLI) or an easy-to-use web-based device manager (WBM). However, the Traffic Anomaly Detector WBM supports only a subset of the CLI of the Traffic Anomaly Detector.

Configuring the Traffic Anomaly Detector

The Traffic Anomaly Detector must be bootstrapped or configured to allow web-based access to the device. The following CLI commands allow web-based access:

```
service wbm
permit wbm ip-addr [ip-mask]
```

ip-addr [*ip-mask*] is the IP address of the host the launches the web browser.

Launch the web browser and type the following:

```
https://detector-ip-addr
```

detector-ip-addr is the IP address of the Detector.

Enter the username and password for the administrative rights to configure the Traffic Anomaly Detector, and you will see the homepage of the Traffic Anomaly Detector WBM, as shown in Figure 2-3. The Traffic Anomaly Detector WBM features a Detector Summary, which displays the average, minimum, maximum, and current level of network traffic through the Traffic Anomaly Detector in bits per second (bps).

Figure 2-3   *Traffic Anomaly Detector WBM Homepage*

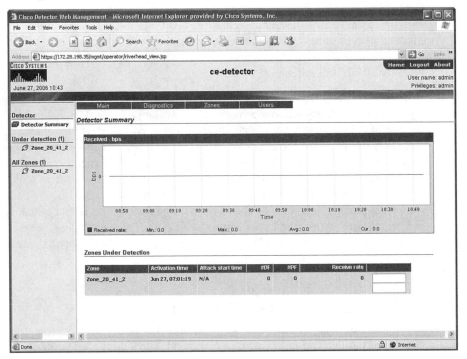

Zone Creation

The Traffic Anomaly Detector attempts to detect a DDoS attack against a particular zone. You can create a zone under the Zones tab by selecting **Create Zone**. Figure 2-4 shows an example of the Create Zone configuration panel.

You can give a zone a name and template, which contains a list of default DDoS mitigation policies templates to be constructed and tuned for the zone. Default templates are provided to create a base DDoS protection coverage. You can copy and edit these default configuration policies to provide customized configuration policies for more advanced attack protection.

Zones can be created with either a DETECTOR_zone template or a GUARD_zone template. A zone that is created with GUARD_zone template has the ability to be automatically synchronized with the Guard. DETECTOR_zone templates are designed for use when zone information does not need to be synchronized with the Guard.

Figure 2-4   *Create Zone Configuration*

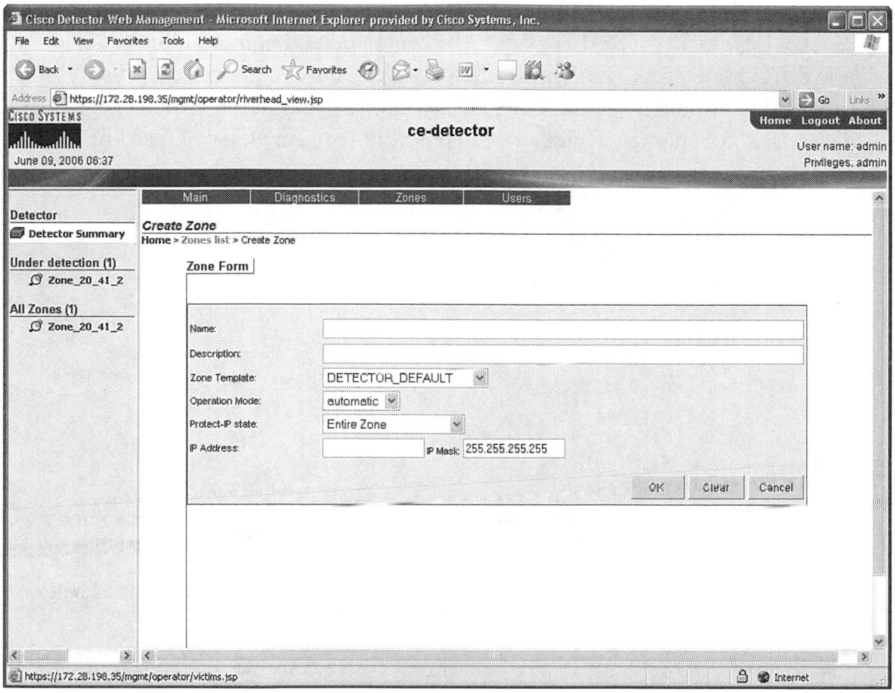

The Traffic Anomaly Detector can inform the admin of a potential DDoS attack, or a Traffic Anomaly Detector can automatically inform or trigger the Guard to mitigate the attack. Select the automatic operation mode for the Traffic Anomaly Detector to inform the Guard to trigger or automatically protect against the known attack so that the network can be self-defending against a DDoS attack without user intervention.

CAUTION   A self-defending network is a very powerful concept. However, be aware that a self-defending network can automatically configure network devices, reroute and deny network traffic, and may result in false positives. A *false positive* is valid network traffic that was dropped, delayed, or otherwise affected due to an incorrect classification that the valid network traffic was in fact part of a network attack.

To configure the IP address of the remote Guard that will protect the Traffic Anomaly Detector's zone, you must use CLI. Example 2-1 shows an example of a base Traffic Anomaly Detector configuration file that details how to configure the IP address of the remote Guard for the Traffic Anomaly Detector. Network connections between the Traffic Anomaly Detector and the remote Guard are secured with Secure Shell (SSH) or Secure Socket Layer (SSL). SSH keys must be generated and applied to both devices to complete the SSH connection. The Traffic Anomaly Detector can generate a private-public SSH key pair and distribute its public key to every Guard listed in the remote-guards list. Multiple Cisco Traffic Anomaly Detectors can report to the same Cisco Guard for a distributed architecture.

Example 2-1 *CLI Configuration of the Cisco Traffic Anomaly Detector Service Module*

```
hostname ce-detector
timezone America/Los_Angeles

history logs 7
history reports 30
no export packet-dump
boot reactivate-zones
tacacs-server timeout 0
tacacs-server key (null)
no tacacs-server first-hit
aaa authentication login local
aaa authentication enable local
no aaa authorization exec tacacs+
username riverhead dynamic encrypted $1$LVZopVja$8kSY10uykJaSYT325wDDk/
username cleanpipes adm1n09 encrypted 18KLWZvg0DP02
enable password level admin encrypted 18xVodWfkJfOk
enable password level config encrypted 84QiLbAV5gfOA
enable password level dynamic encrypted 161R6GsPeIPWs

snmp community public

snmp trap-dest 172.28.198.22 public debugging
interface eth0
  ip address 172.28.198.35 255.255.255.0
  mtu 1500
  no shutdown
exit
interface giga0
  mtu 1500
  no shutdown
exit
interface giga1
  mtu 1500
  no shutdown
exit

default-gateway 172.28.198.1
service ntp
service wbm
service internode-comm
service snmp-trap
```

Example 2-1 *CLI Configuration of the Cisco Traffic Anomaly Detector Service Module (Continued)*

```
permit wbm  17.28.198.100
permit ssh  17.28.198.100
permit internode-comm 172.28.198.34

ntp server 171.68.10.150

logging host 172.28.198.22
logging trap informational
logging facility local7


zone Zone_20_41_2 GUARD_DEFAULT interactive

 no learning-params periodic-action
 learning-params threshold-selection max-thresholds
 learning-params threshold-tuned
 learning-params sync accept
 learning-params sync remote-activate
 no packet-dump auto-capture
 packet-dump disk-space 2048
 ip address 20.41.2.0 255.255.255.0

 remote-guard ssl 172.28.198.34
 protect-ip-state  entire-zone
 no bypass-filter *
 no flex-content-filter *



admin@ce-detector-conf#conf t
admin@ce-detector-conf#remote-guard
  ssh                 :  Secure shell
  ssl                 :  Secure socket layer

admin@ce-detector-conf#remote-guard ssl
  <remote-guard-address>:  IP address in dotted-decimal notation (A.B.C.D)
```

Traffic Anomaly Detector Zone Filters

Zone filters enable mirrored network traffic to be managed by the Detector. Zone filters enable the Traffic Anomaly Detector to drop traffic prior to inspection by the Traffic Anomaly Detector. Zone filters also enable the Traffic Anomaly Detector to analyze network traffic for spikes or anomalies and notify the Guard of these network traffic abnormalities. There are four types of filters:

- **User**—User filters are assigned to a Zone that is created with the GUARD_zone template. User filters are used to provide a first layer of defense against the attack until the Guard has analyzed the attack and until the Guard can create custom, dynamic filters for the network attack.

- **Bypass**—Bypass filters restrict certain network traffic flows from being directed to the Detector.

- **Flex**—Flex filters support the ability to count a specific traffic flow.

- **Dynamic**—The Detector creates dynamic filters as the result of an analysis of a traffic flow. The dynamic filter is the mechanism to activate a remote Guard to protect a zone, or an IP address in a zone, in the event of a detected DDoS attack for a specific IP traffic flow. Dynamic filters are temporary and are expected to expire at the end of a DDoS attack.

You can configure user, bypass, and flex filters with the Traffic Anomaly Detector WBM. You can create these filters by selecting the Configuration tab for a specific Zone.

Policy Template

A *policy template* is a collection of information that is leveraged during the learning phase of the zone. The policy template provides the basis for creating the zone's detection policies after the normal traffic baseline is established during the learning phase. To configure a policy template for a zone, go to Configuration > Policy template as shown in Figure 2-5.

Figure 2-5   *Policy Template Configuration*

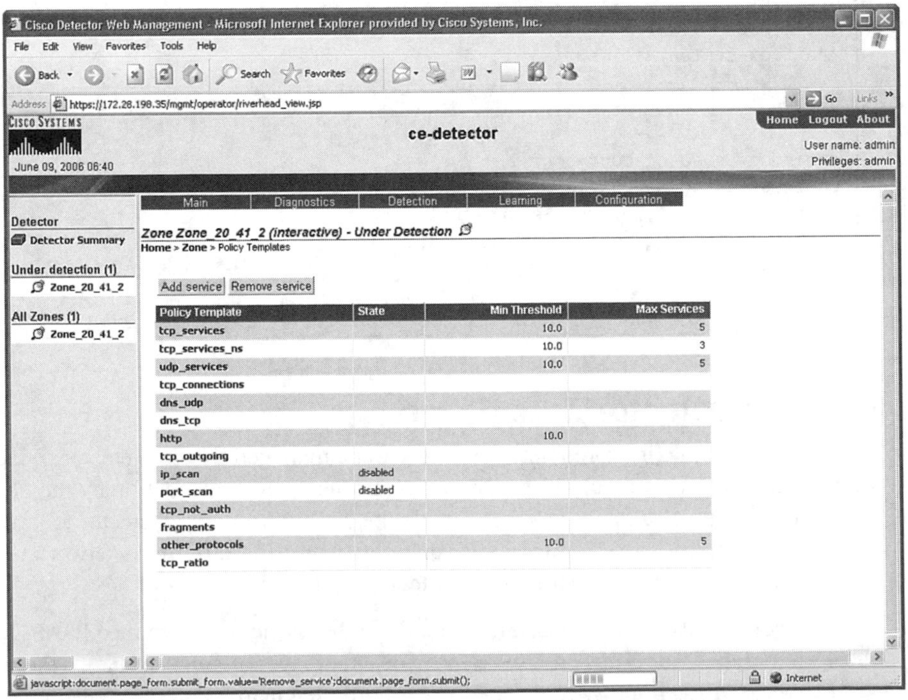

You can select and edit the policy templates. The primary parameters or options for each policy template are

- **State**—State allows the user to enable or disable/turn-off a policy template. It is strongly cautioned that disabling/turning-off a default policy template can compromise the DDoS protection of a zone because there may be no policies to protect the network traffic that would have been specified in the policy template.

- **Minimum threshold**—Minimum threshold refers to packets-per-second (pps) or total number of network connections. The Guard will not create a dynamic filter to mitigate an attack until the traffic flow exceeds the minimum threshold.

- **Maximum services**—Maximum services refers to the number of port numbers or service ports that are protected by the Guard for that policy template. Additional memory on the Traffic Anomaly Detector is required for each additional service in the policy templates for each Zone.

Learning Phase

A zone must enter a learning phase in order to establish a baseline of normal network traffic and to provide a mechanism to construct the zone's active policies from the base policy template. The learning phase consists of two processes:

- Policy construction
- Threshold tuning

In the policy construction phase, zone policies are created from the base template. It is recommended that the policy construction phase run for at least two hours to ensure a proper baseline.

The second phase is the threshold-tuning phase. During this tuning phase, the Traffic Anomaly Detector creates a minimum threshold value for the relevant zone policies. This threshold value is used to indicate the minimum level of network traffic for specific network flows that would indicate a potential DDoS attack on the zone. It is recommended that the threshold-tuning phase run for at least 24 hours to improve the computation of the minimum threshold values for each service that will constitute a possible DDoS attack. Zones that were created with the GUARD_zone template cannot initiate the policy construction phase from the Traffic Anomaly Detector. You can initiate the policy construction and the phases for zones created with the DETECTER_zone template through the Traffic Anomaly Detector WBM, as shown in Figure 2-6.

Figure 2-6 *Initiating the Learning Phase*

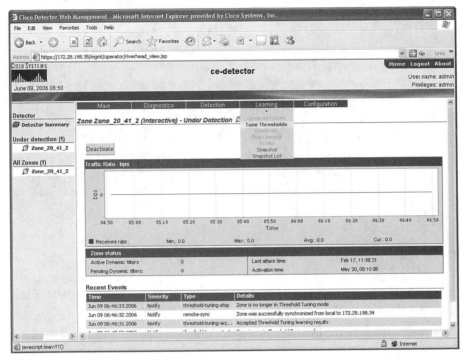

Detecting and Reporting Traffic Anomalies

After you have completed the learning phase, constructed zone policies, and tuned the threshold values, you can enable the zone to detect a traffic anomaly or potential DDoS attack. Figure 2-7 shows an example of the Detection tab in the Traffic Anomaly Detector WBM. Figure 2-7 also displays the location to view any generated dynamic filters. Dynamic filters are created by the Traffic Anomaly Detector during the detection of a potential DDoS attack. These dynamic filters created by the Traffic Anomaly Detector are used to create a syslog or are used as a trigger to activate the remote Guard to scrub the network traffic.

The Traffic Anomaly Detector WBM also offers extensive diagnostic information, including counters and attack reports. Figure 2-8 shows an example of an attack report, which indicates what attacks were detected and when they were detected. Attack reports can also be exported in text and XML format.

Figure 2-7 *Zone Detection*

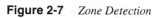

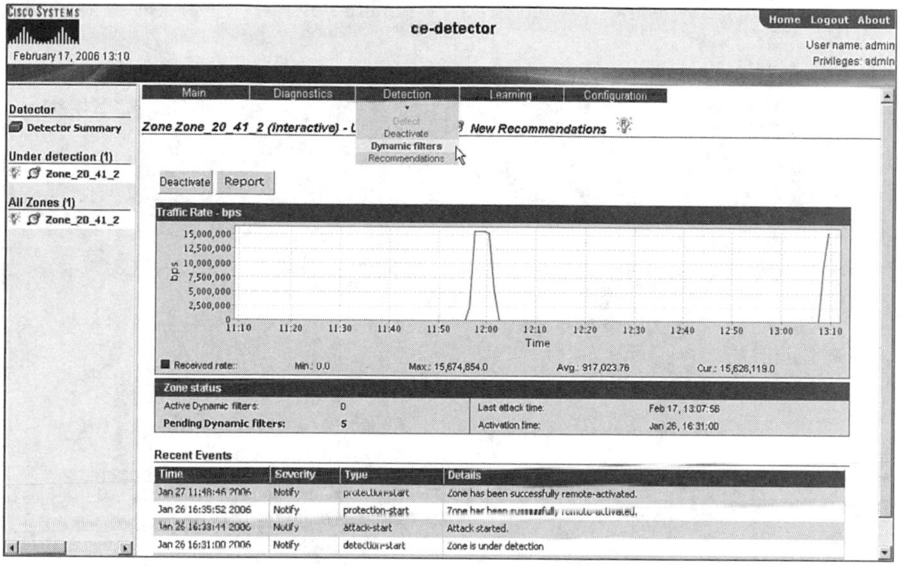

Figure 2-8 *Attack Reports*

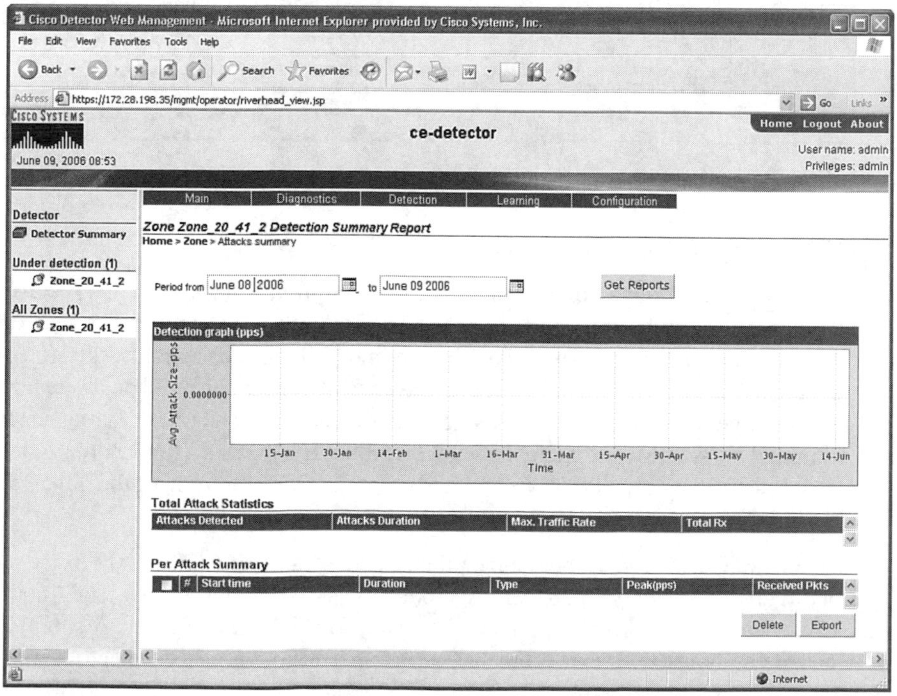

Figure 2-9 shows an example of the diagnostic event log with details on Traffic Anomaly Detector activity, warnings, and pending dynamic filters.

Figure 2-9 *Event Logs*

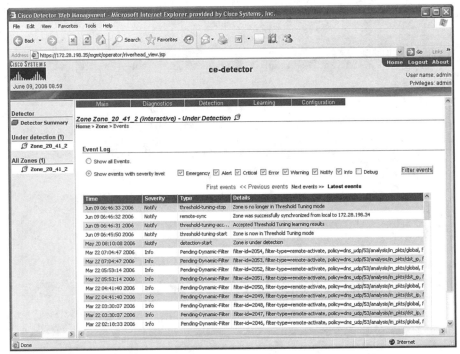

Configuring Cisco Guard

The Cisco Guard is the component of the DDoS mitigation solution that receives the network attack traffic for a zone from the Traffic Anomaly Detector. The Guard scrubs or removes the attack traffic and forwards or reinjects the good (nonattack) traffic back to the destination zone. The Guard is often deployed upstream at the ISP/backbone layer and can protect large network segments. A single Guard can protect more than one zone simultaneously as long as there are no overlapping IP addresses in multiple zones. A native self-protection mechanism is also contained in the Guard to protect the Guard itself from becoming the target of a DDoS attack.

The Guard is available as both an appliance and a Catalyst 6500/7600 service module. A picture of the Anomaly Guard service module is shown in Figure 2-10. The Anomaly Guard service module, unlike the appliance, contains no onboard interfaces. A single Catalyst chassis can house both the Anomaly Guard and Traffic Anomaly Detector service module.

Figure 2-10 *Catalyst 6500/7600 Anomaly Guard Service Module*

Source: Cisco Systems, Inc.

Like the Traffic Anomaly Detector, the Guard also features an easy-to-use WBM. The Guard's WBM is similar in philosophy to that of the Traffic Anomaly Detector's WBM in that the Guard WBM supports only a subset of the CLI that is implemented on the Guard. The Guard WBM features focus around the areas of zone configuration, status, and reports. Other Guard features, including zone traffic diversion, must be configured with the CLI since they are not supported in the Guard WBM.

Configuring and using the Guard includes the following:

- Bootstrapping
- Zones creation and synchronization
- Zone filters
- Zone traffic diversion
- Learning Phase
  - Policy construction
  - Threshold tuning
- Activating zone protection
- Attack reports

Bootstrapping

The process to bootstrap and initialize the Guard is similar to the process described previously for the Traffic Anomaly Detector in the Configuring the Traffic Anomaly Detector section. The Guard must have an interface configured, and the WBM service should be started and permitted with the Guard CLI in order to be managed by the Guard WBM.

Zone Creation and Synchronization

The zone that is to be protected must be either configured on the Guard or synchronized from the Traffic Anomaly Detector. Zones that are configured on the Guard can be configured in a manner similar to that described previously in the Zone Creation section for the Traffic Anomaly Detector. However, many users will instead want to synchronize the zones that were already created on the Traffic Anomaly Detector using the GUARD_zone template. This process to synchronize the zones from the Traffic Anomaly Detector must be performed with Guard CLI because the zone synchronization feature is not supported in the Guard WBM.

Cisco Guard Zone Filters

The Guard features user, bypass, flex, and dynamic filters. These filter types were described previously in this chapter in the section "Traffic Anomaly Detector Zone Filters." In the event of a suspected DDoS attack, the Guard generates dynamic filters. These dynamic filters are temporary and expire after the end of the DDoS attack. These dynamic filters instruct the Traffic Anomaly Detector on what action to perform on the suspected network attack traffic.

The Guard can also create a default set of user filters to provide a base of protection until additional dynamic filters are created after the analysis of network attack traffic. The user filters are displayed in Figure 2-11, which illustrates the user filters for a specific zone on the Guard.

Figure 2-11 *Guard User Filter*

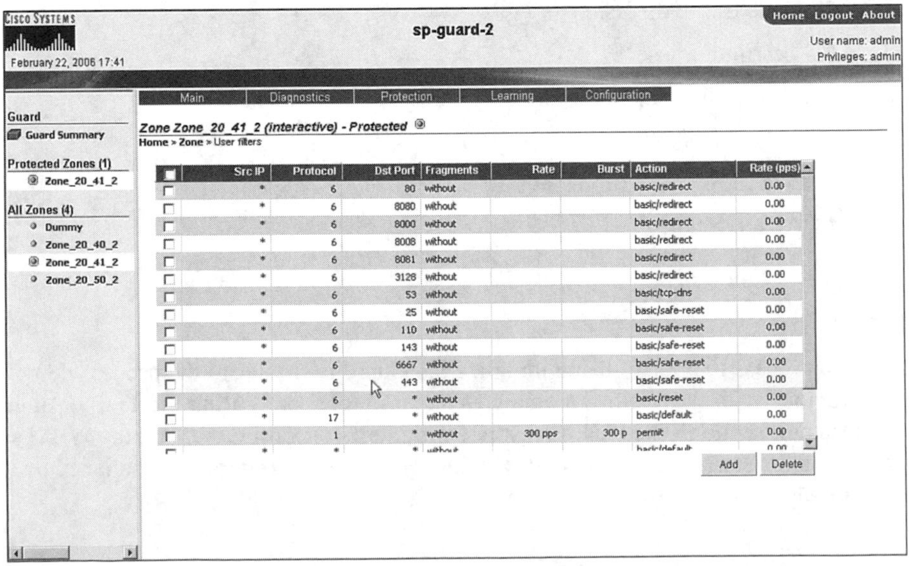

User filters can also be created manually on the Guard for a user to customize how the Guard should process a specific network traffic flow. Figure 2-12 provides an example of the options available when configuring a User Filter. The options for the User Filter include the following:

- **Source IP**—Includes any wildcard (*)
- **Source Subnet**—Select from drop-down
- **Protocol**—Includes any wildcard (*)
- **Dst Port**—Refers to the Destination Port (*)
- **Fragments**—Includes With, Without, or *
- **Rate**—Limits traffic to specified rate
- **Burst**—Refers to the Burst traffic limit
- **Action**—Includes parameters to permit traffic flow to avoid Guard antispoofing and antizombie protection, authenticate, and drop traffic

Figure 2-12 *User Filter Creation*

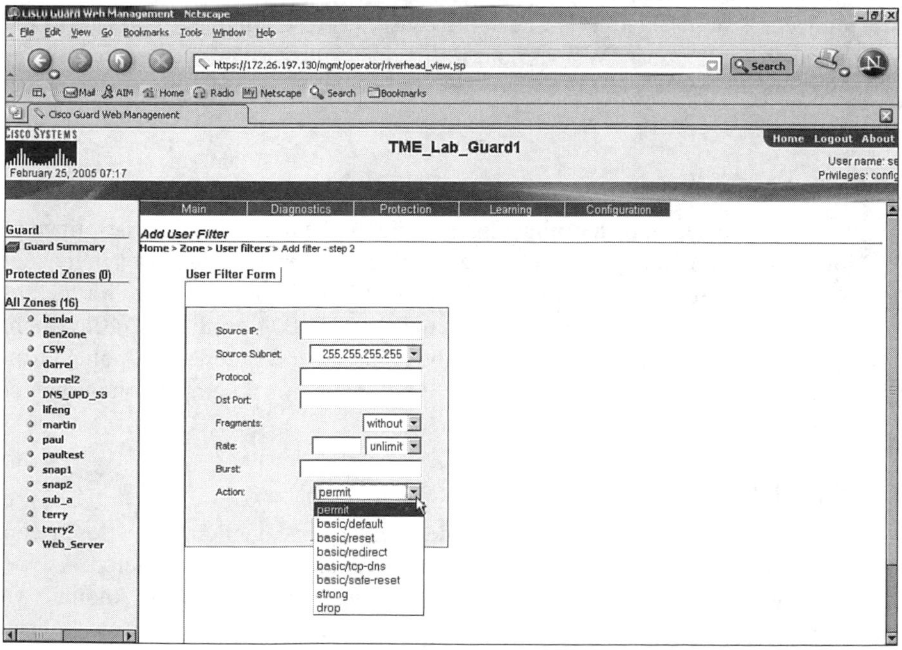

Zone Traffic Diversion

Zone traffic diversion is composed of two phases:

- Divert potential DDoS traffic destined to the zone.
- Inject the scrubbed or good network traffic back from the Guard to the zone.

In the first phase, BGP routing updates are one of the most common mechanisms used to divert attack traffic from the router to the Guard for scrubbing. The Guard achieves this traffic diversion by sending a BGP update to the router to indicate that the next-hop for the zone is the Guard itself. This BGP announcement from the Guard contains a more specific prefix to ensure that the Guard is the best path for the next-hop to the zone. This BGP announcement from the Guard is often sent with a no export and no community string option to ensure that this BGP announcement is not propagated to other routes within the network.

For the second phase of traffic diversion, several traffic forwarding mechanisms, including next-hop router discovery, policy-based routing, VPN routing and forwarding (VRF), VLANs and GRE/IPIP tunnels, can be used to inject the scrubbed traffic back to the destination zone. Both the process to divert the network attack traffic to the Guard and reinject the scrubbed traffic back to the zone must be configured with CLI as they are not supported by the Guard WBM. Zone traffic diversion must be configured with CLI prior to initiating the learning phase for policy creation and threshold tuning.

Learning Phase

The Guard undergoes a learning phase similar to the learning phase described previously for the Traffic Anomaly Detector. The learning phase is composed of a policy construction phase and a threshold-tuning phase. Figure 2-13 displays the policies for the dns_tcp and dns_udp services for a specific zone on the Guard WBM. Both the Traffic Anomaly Detector and the Guard WBM feature the ability to cross-launch the policy display in the Guard and Traffic Anomaly Detector WBM for additional comparison purposes.

Activating Zone Protection

A zone must be placed into protect mode after the zone configuration, policy construction, threshold tuning, and traffic diversion configuration has been completed. A zone can be automatically placed into protect mode by a trigger from the Traffic Anomaly Detector during a DDoS attack. The trigger from the Traffic Anomaly Detector can indicate whether the entire zone should be placed into protect mode or if a specific IP address in a zone should be placed into protect mode by the creation of a subzone. You can also manually place a zone in protect mode through the Protection tab in the Guard WBM, as shown in Figure 2-14.

Figure 2-13 *Display of Policy for a Zone on the Guard*

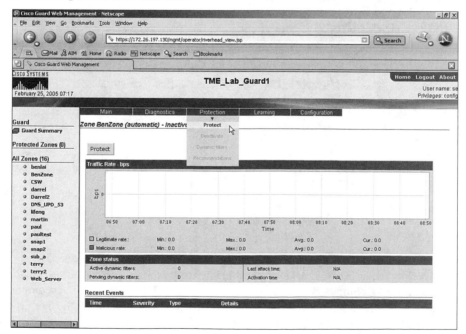

Figure 2-14 *Placing a Zone in Protect Mode*

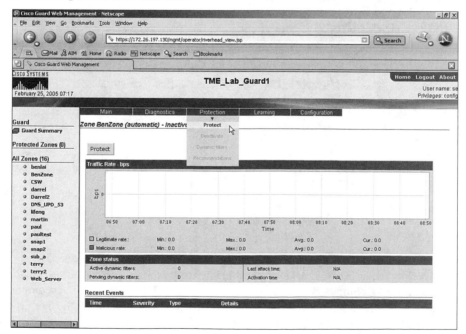

Generating Attack Reports

You can generate an extensive list of attack reports from the Guard WMB. These attack reports include metrics on the number of mitigated attacks and a per-attack summary with a breakdown of legitimate versus malicious network traffic. Figure 2-15 displays the beginning of an attack report with total attack statistics.

Figure 2-15 *Total Attack Statistics*

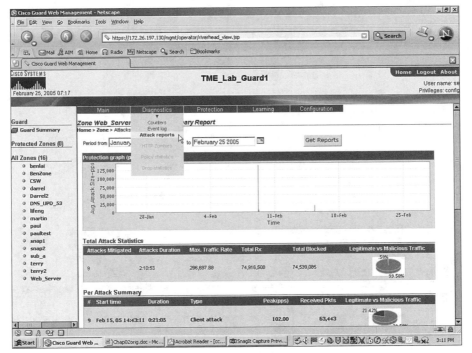

Like the Traffic Anomaly Detector, these attack reports on the Guard are also exportable in both text and XML format.

Summary

DDoS attacks are an attempt to prevent valid users from using network resources by flooding the network. This flooding of the network is often performed by hundreds or thousands of compromised zombie computers. Cisco DDoS mitigation is composed of two key components: the Traffic Anomaly Detector and the Guard. Both the Traffic Anomaly Detector and the Guard have a subset of their CLI that is managed by a Traffic Anomaly Detector WBM and a Guard WBM.

Figure 3-2 *Antispoofing/uRPF Configuration*

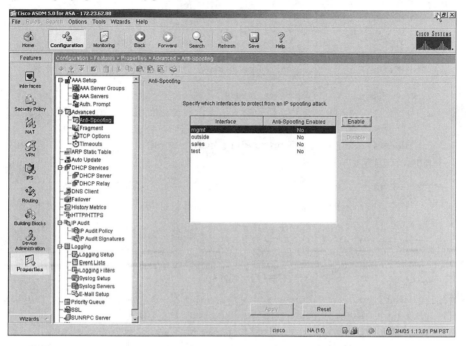

Intrusion Prevention Service

Cisco ASA supports an inline Intrusion Prevention Security Service on the Advanced Inspection and Protection Security Services Module (AIP-SSM). The Intrusion Prevention module provides the ability to identify and drop the IP packets of an active network attack. The actual configuration of the IPS signatures is not shown in the base ASA configuration file, which can be displayed with telnet/SSH or ASDM. The existence of an AIPSSM module is indicated in the **show module** telnet/SSH CLI command as shown in Example 3-1.

Example 3-1 *The **show module** Command*

```
asdm-89/admin# show module

Mod Card Type                                             Model              Serial No.
--- -------------------------------------------------- ------------------ -----------
  0 ASA 5520 Adaptive Security Appliance                 ASA5520            P3000000192
  1 ASA 5500 Series Security Services Module-10          ASA-SSM-10         JAB0818067A

Mod MAC Address Range                   Hw Version  Fw Version  Sw Version
--- ----------------------------------- ----------- ----------- ---------------
  0 000b.fcf8.c623 to 000b.fcf8.c627    1.0         1.0(10)0    7.2(0)47
  1 000b.fcf8.0156 to 000b.fcf8.0156    1.0         1.0(10)0    6.0(0.51)S212.0
```

continues

Example 3-1 *The* **show module** *Command (Continued)*

```
Mod SSM Application Name            Status          SSM Application Version
--- ----------------------------- --------------- ------------------------
  1 IPS                            Up              6.0(0.51)S212.0

Mod Status              Data Plane Status    Compatibility
--- ------------------- -------------------- -------------
  0 Up Sys              Not Applicable
  1 Up                  Up
```

The process to configure IPS inspection of network traffic with the AIP-SSM with ASDM includes the following:

- Launch ASDM for IPS Configuration
- Configure service policy rules to specify a class of traffic for IPS inspection
- Define the IPS signature set for inspection of network traffic

Launch ASDM for IPS Configuration

IPS Configuration is simple and intuitive with ASDM. You initiate IPS Configuration by selecting **Configuration** from the top panel and **IPS** from the left panel. The AIP-SSM module can be separately managed from the ASA chassis and has its own IP address. In addition to ASDM, you can also manage the AIP module by telnet/SSH directly to the IP address of the IPS module. You can also centrally manage the ASA AIP-SSM with the Cisco Security Manager.

Cisco Security Manager is Cisco's centralized security manager that you can use to manage or configure security components on ASA, IPS, and router devices. Cisco Security Manager is a very strategic element in the Cisco security portfolio. Cisco Security Manager is discussed in detail in Chapter 9, "Cisco Security Manager."

You can display or view the CLI file of the AIP-SSM, which can be created with ASDM, by issuing the **session module** *slot* command from the base ASA platform. ASDM will indicate the IP address of the AIP-SSM automatically after you select **Configure** and **IPS** from the main ASDM homepage. The AIP-SSM module also supports a separate username and password. Figure 3-3 shows an example of how to access the GUI display of the AIP-SSM module configuration from ASDM.